PVT. WARS

A COMEDY IN ONE ACT
BY JAMES McLURE

DRAMATISTS
PLAY SERVICE
INC.

PVT. WARS was presented by Michael Harvey and Peter A. Bobley, in association with Columbia Pictures, at the Century Theatre, in New York City, on June 7, 1979. It was directed by Garland Wright; the scenery was by John Arnone; costumes were by Giva Taylor, and the lighting was by Frances Aronson. The associate producers were Stewart F. Lane and Jack Tantleff. The cast, in order of appearance, was as follows:

WOODRUFF GATELY .... Gregory Grove

SILVIO .... Tony Campisi

NATWICK .... Clifford Fetters

The play takes place on an outdoor terrace of an army veterans hospital.

The time, the present, during several days and one night.

PVT. WARS was produced as a staged reading at Actors Theatre of Louisville, Louisville, Kentucky.

In the New York production the transition speeches were tape recorded.

CHARACTERS

WOODRUFF GATELY, a young southerner. Childlike, mentally slow but not stupid. The kind of man who at age 30 might chase a fire engine to see where it was going.

SILVIO, Italian American. Street-wise, tough but not cruel.

NATWICK, a young man from Long Island. Intelligent, spoiled. He should never have been in the armed forces.

PVT. WARS

A Sunny day. Gately at the table fixing a radio. Pause. Silvio enters hurriedly. Pause. He notices Gately.

SILVIO. What the hell you doing?
GATELY. Fixing a radio.
SILVIO. What the hell for?
GATELY. It's for Hinson.
SILVIO. What's Hinson need a radio for? I need a radio more than Hinson.
GATELY. Why?
SILVIO. Hinson doesn't have any arms or legs.
GATELY. Yes, but you move around too much. This has to be plugged in.
SILVIO. I'll get an extension cord. (*Pause.*) One thing I've noticed about you. You concentrate and you do things slowly. How do you account for this?
GATELY. Hard drugs.
SILVIO. I see.
GATELY. It's for my nerves.
SILVIO. Do the drugs help?
GATELY. Oh yes. I hardly have any nerves left at all. (*Pause.*) Could you hand me that piece of wire? I want to do a good job of this. I figure if I do a good job of this radio, they may let me out of here.
SILVO. You can get out any time you want.
GATELY. I know that.
SILVIO. But you figure, if you finish that radio, they'll let you out.
GATELY. Sure. It's all part of the Free Enterprise system.
SILVIO. I see. (*Silvio refers to a pocket notebook.*) OK, I gotta go.
GATELY. OK.

5

SILVIO. Yeah, there's some orderly over in C Ward givin' those guys a lotta shit. Can you believe that? So—I gotta go.
GATELY. OK.
SILVIO. So, uh, you here a lot? You hang out here?
GATELY. Yeah.
SILVIO. You're Gately, right?
GATELY. Yeah.
SILVIO. Tell you what. I'll see you later. (*Silvio exits. Gately watches him go.*)

Blackout

Transition 1. Over intercom.
Atkins and Johnson wanted in C Ward immediately. Disturbance between patient and personnel. It's Silvio again. Jesus Christ.

SCENE TWO. I Don't Want To Talk About It.

Gately fixing radio. Natwick enters in robe and slippers, carrying a newspaper. He is visibly upset. He sits, opens paper, covering his face. He lowers paper.

NATWICK. I don't want to talk about it.
GATELY. What?
NATWICK. I don't want to talk about it.
GATELY. What don't you want to talk about?
NATWICK. Look, I said I didn't want to talk about it, OK?
GATELY. OK. (*Pause. Gately begins to whistle. "Zippity-Doo-Dah."*)
NATWICK. Do you mind? I'm trying to read.
GATELY. Natwick, if you won't tell me what not to talk about, how do you know I might not *accidentally* start talking about it?
NATWICK. (*Confidentially.*) The odds are ten trillion to one against it.
GATELY. Oh.
NATWICK. (*Darkly.*) But I don't even want to take *that* chance. (*Pause.*)
GATELY. I'll bet I could guess what it is.

6

NATWICK. (*Amused.*) Don't even waste your time. (*Slight pause.*)

GATELY. Is it something that just happened to you?

NATWICK. (*Guarding.*) What?

GATELY. Did someone do something to you?

NATWICK. (*Sinking.*) I don't want—

GATELY. Was it staff?

NATWICK. One down, two to go.

GATELY. Was it someone in the ward?

NATWICK. Two down, one to go.

GATELY. Was it Gleason?

NATWICK. (*Exulting.*) Three down, none to—

GATELY. Was it Silvio?

NATWICK. What?

GATELY. Was it Silvio? (*Silvio enters with a smile to suggest he has eaten Natwick's first-born.*)

SILVIO. Hello, Gately.

GATELY. Hello, Silvio.

SILVIO. (*Pause.*) Hello, Natwick.

Blackout

Transition 2. Natwick letter.

Dear Mother. There is a guy here named Silvio. Mother, I think there is something very wrong with him. He's violent and terribly anti-social. I don't know why they let people like this in the Army. Your loving son, Natwick.

SCENE THREE. Underwear.

Gately fixing radio.
Silvio standing looking off, intently, into distance.

SILVIO. Would you look at that. Would you look at that. (*Pause.*) Hey, beautiful! Hey, gorgeous! Turn around! Ta-dah! (*Silvio unties robe, flashes, reties robe. Smiles contentedly. Silvio slips underpants on underneath robe.*) I don't know. I like the floppy kind of underwear. It gives you more of a sense of freedom, you know? You can flop around. One has mobility. (*Pause.*)

GATELY. That's very good. You could go on TV. Advertise floppy underwear.

SILVIO. Yeah, if I wanted to I could. I ain't got the time though. But I could if I wanted to, y'know, because I believe in floppy underwear. (*Pause.*) Only one drawback to floppy underwear.

GATELY. What's that?

SILVIO. They make you feel like an old man. That's the trouble with life, Gately. You may find something you like, but if it makes you feel like an old man—what's the point? (*Pause.*) You get my point? (*Pause.*) You know another thing makes you feel like an old man?

GATELY. An old woman?

SILVIO. Garters.

GATELY. You're right.

SILVIO. You damn right I'm right. I had to wear garters to my brother's wedding.

GATELY. Did it make you feel like an old man?

SILVIO. You damn right. Besides the garters didn't work.

GATELY. Maybe you were wearing the wrong kinda socks.

SILVIO. Maybe you're right.

GATELY. What kind did you wear?

SILVIO. Athletic socks.

GATELY. You wore athletic socks to your brother's wedding?

SILVIO. You see, Gately, I'm Catholic.

GATELY. Did the Pope make you do it?

SILVIO. Don't get cute, Gately. It was his second marriage. OK? First time around I wear black socks. Second time around I figured, fuck it. You see, Gately, I respect the state of holy matrimony.

GATELY. So do I.

SILVIO. And I respect the holy Catholic Church.

GATELY. So do I.

SILVIO. I know you do. Let's shake on it. (*They stand and shake on it.*) Now, I'd like to return for a minute, if I may, to the subject of underwear.

GATELY. All right.

SILVIO. Now then. Floppy versus tight. Me? I don't see any comparison. 'Cause, I mean, in terms of underwear, what is a man looking for?

GATELY. Fashion?

SILVIO. Certainly fashion. I mean, you're with a chick, right?

8

You don't want to take off your pants, right? and have her laugh at your underwear?

GATELY. She might though, if you're wearing flopping underwear.

SILVIO. That's why you gotta get a good pattern. Take a look at these. (*He opens robe.*) Are these smart or what.

GATELY. They're pretty smart.

SILVIO. My sister sent me these.

GATELY. Your sister's got good taste in men's underwear.

SILVIO. Of course.

GATELY. Kinda makes you wonder though.

SILVIO. What?

GATELY. How you sister got such good taste in men's underwear.

SILVIO. (*Pointing finger.*) Hey. Watch it. (*Pause.*) OK. So the way I see it. A guy needs fashion. And a guy needs mobility. And outside of that there's nothing else a guy needs.

GATELY. Snugness.

SILVIO. (*Unsettled.*) What?

GATELY. Snugness.

SILVIO. Uh, oh. I think I hear the voice of a tight underwear man here.

GATELY. Well, a guy doesn't always want floppy underwear.

SILVIO. Now wait a minute.

GATELY. Underwear are like socks.

SILVIO. Stop. I don't know if I can let that get by.

GATELY. You don't want your socks slipping down. A man wants snug socks.

SILVIO. (*Pondering.*) Socks are like underwear. (*Pause.*) What kind you wearing?

GATELY. Black ones.

SILVIO. (*Troubled.*) Oh yeah?

GATELY. Yeah.

SILVIO. Are they tight?

GATELY. (*Underneath table, wiggles his foot.*) They're pretty tight.

SILVIO. They're not black silk are they?

GATELY. Black polyester, I think. But all mine got holes in them.

SILVIO. Of course they've got holes. It's a modern convenience.

GATELY. I've got holes on the balls.

SILVIO. Holes on the balls!

GATELY. I've gotta get some new ones.

9

SILVIO. I guess so.

GATELY. But I've got a problem. I got different sizes. My left is bigger than my right.

SILVIO. Well, how much difference can there be.

GATELY. About an inch. One's about nine inches long.

SILVIO. What!

GATELY. The other's about 10 inches.

SILVIO. Nine and 10 inches?

GATELY. Yeah. I was born that way.

SILVIO. Jesus Christ. What about . . . you know . . . Mr. In-Between.

GATELY. What?

SILVIO. Never mind. (*Pause.*)

GATELY. I find though, if I buy, oh nine to say 11, that fits everything.

SILVIO. You're not talking about around are you?

GATELY. Hell no! I'm talking about length. What's the matter, Silvio?

SILVIO. I don't want to talk about it. (*Silvio sinks into darkest depression. Natwick enters. Sits.*)

GATELY. Hello, Natwick.

NATWICK. I don't want to talk about it. (*Pause. Notices Silvio's depression.*) What's the matter with Little Mary Sunshine?

GATELY. He doesn't want to talk about it.

NATWICK. Very intelligent of him.

GATELY. Pretty soon I'll be talking to myself around here. Say, Natwick. What size feet do you have?

NATWICK. About a nine. Ten.

GATELY. Can I borrow some socks. Mine are wearing out on the balls of my feet.

NATWICK. Do you still have athlete's foot?

SILVIO. What?

NATWICK. Does he still have athlete's foot?

SILVIO. You were talking about the balls of your feet.

GATELY. Of course.

SILVIO. Oh, you were talking about socks!

GATELY. Yes.

SILVIO. Oh. You hear that, Natwick? He was talking about socks.

NATWICK. Yes. I'm overwhelmed.

10

SILVIO. Oh. Wow. Great. That's great. That's terrific. Jesus, that's a relief. Fucking socks. (*Exits relieved.*)
NATWICK. What did you say about socks?
GATELY. I don't know. (*They took off to where Silvio has exited. Gately returns to radio. Natwick reads paper.*)
NATWICK. Why are you still fixing that radio?
GATELY. For Hinson.
NATWICK. Hinson's dead.
GATELY. How can he be dead? I saw him just yesterday. He was perfectly all right. He didn't have any arms or legs, but he was all right.
NATWICK. He died last night.
GATELY. One day he's alive, the next he's dead.
NATWICK. That's life. (*Pause.*)
GATELY. But this is a hospital.
NATWICK. That's the way it is in a hospital. Either you get better or you die or you rot. (*Gately, stunned, gets up, walks away from table. Turns. Looks at radio.*) Look at it this way. At least you don't have to waste your time on that stupid radio. Gately, we all die sooner or later. You know, Gately, in many ways we're alike.
GATELY. We're nothing alike.
NATWICK. Of coure we are. We're both intelligent and sensitive.
GATELY. Am I?
NATWICK. Well, you're sensitive.
GATELY. Am I?
NATWICK. You'd have to be either sensitive or just plain stupid to fix a radio for Hinson.
GATELY. Why?
NATWICK. Everyone knew Hinson was going to die. (*Gately returns to radio. He begins work.*) Gately, what are you doing?
GATELY. Fixing the radio.
NATWICK. Gately, Hinson's dead.
GATELY. I know that.
NATWICK. Gately, don't be a fool.
GATELY. Someone else can use it.
NATWICK. You're deluding yourself.
GATELY. No I'm not. If I fix this radio, they'll let me out of here.
NATWICK. You can get out anytime you want to.
GATELY. You see, Natwick, every cloud has a silver lining.

NATWICK. Yes. But that's just what it is.

GATELY. What?

NATWICK. A lining. You takes out that lining, you know what you've got?

GATELY. What?

NATWICK. A cloud. A very dark, dangerous cloud.

SILVIO. (*Entering.*) Hello, Gately.

GATELY. Hello, Silvio.

SILVIO. Natwick, go fuck yourself. (*Natwick gapes and exits.*) One thing about Natwick—you tell him to go do something and by God, he goes and does it. (*Gately returns to radio. Silvio seated.*) Gately, I've been thinking of buying a kilt.

GATELY. A kilt?

SILVIO. Yeah, it's a kind of dress that guys in Scotland wear. (*Pause.*) It's kinda like a cheerleader's skirt.

GATELY. If you want a cheerleader's skirt, why don't you just buy a cheerleader's skirt.

SILVIO. I don't want no cheerleader's skirt.

GATELY. Oh.

SILVIO. What would I do with a cheerleader's skirt?

GATELY. I have no idea.

SILVIO. Hey, wait a minute. You think I want to wear a girl's skirt. You think that? Is that what you think?

GATELY. Look, I don't care—

SILVIO. Look, I don't care that you don't care! Who cares!

GATELY. Not me.

SILVIO. Look, I don't want to wear a dress, OK.

GATELY. OK.

SILVIO. I want to wear a kilt. (*Pause.*) Look, I read somewhere that Scots have a very high potency rate. So I said to myself, what have they got that we haven't got?

GATELY. Kilts?

SILVIO. Right. Gately, did you know tight pants weaken the sperm count?

GATELY. They prove that?

SILVIO. They've practically proved that. Gately, picture if you will, an Oregon stream in the spring of the year, the icy waters teaming with salmon. Indians poised, ready to spear them as they spawn. Returning from the sea to a very old place. Now these salmon returning to spawn are called grilse. The grilse overcome

12

incredible obstacles in order to spawn. They have to fight their way past dams and rocks and Indians.
GATELY. Are we still talking about the sperm count?
SILVIO. Gately, I want you to think of your sperm as a salmon.
GATELY. OK.
SILVIO. Think of your sperm as grilse.
GATELY. Grilse!
SILVIO. The sperm is fighting it's way up the vagina! Thrashing on to the spawning grounds! Over rocks and dams and Indians.
GATELY. In the vagina?
SILVIO. But the weak sperm can't make it!
GATELY. They give out?
SILVIO. They poop out. So the sperm pulls over to the side of the vagina. Worse thing they could possibly do!
GATELY. Poor little guys.
SILVIO. In the end all the salmon die. They spawn and they die. And except for the one sperm that fertilizes the egg, this is also the fate of the sperm. (*They both stare out at the world, impressed by the majesty of Silvio's speech.*)
GATELY. Have you ever read Hiawatha?
SILVIO. No.
GATELY. It's full of rocks and rivers and Indians. (*Pause.*) Do you think the sperm know they're gonna die?
SILVIO. At present, Gately, science doesn't know how much the sperm knows. But we can say this about the sperm. (*Thinks.*) It has a helluva sense of direction. (*They both look out.*)

Blackout

Transition 3.   Natwick letter.
Dear Mother, The days pass quickly and I make new friends. So far my favorite person here is a fellow named Gately. We have many pleasant conversations.

SCENE FOUR.   Superior.

NATWICK. Checkmate.
GATELY. Natwick, why do you act so superior?
NATWICK. I don't act superior. I am superior.

GATELY. You're not necessarily superior. I'll tell you something. Silvio's been working on this theory. If you wear kilts your sperm will be more like a grilse's.

NATWICK. What?

GATELY. Grilse are the salmon that fight their way upstream.

NATWICK. No.

GATELY. What?

NATWICK. Grilse are the salmon that fight their way downstream. Grilse are the young salmon, not the mature salmon.

GATELY. What do you call mature salmon?

NATWICK. Salmon.

GATELY. What about kilts? Silvio says we should wear kilts to make us more potent.

NATWICK. Silvio wants to dress like a pervert.

GATELY. Why?

NATWICK. Because he is a pervert. And if we ran around in kilts, we'd be just as perverted as he is.

GATELY. What about the Scots? They run around in kilts. What about them?

NATWICK. They're perverted. (*Pause.*)

GATELY. Have you ever read Hiawatha?

Blackout

Transition 4.

PSYCHIATRIST. Silvio, I want you to relax.

SILVIO. Doc, I am relaxed.

PSYCHIATRIST. I'm here to help you. Now just relax.

SILVIO. I am relaxed.

PSYCHIATRIST. Silvio.

SILVIO. What?

PSYCHIATRIST. If you were *really* relaxed, you'd put down the lamp and get off my desk.

SCENE FIVE. Silvio's Monologue.

SILVIO. I don't know. I have these strange thoughts. They're not violent. (*Pause.*) Some of them are violent. The other day I, uhm, was talking to this old woman. And she was talking and I just

14

wanted to do some outrageous thing to her. Like slap her. Or pull her false teeth out. Or play with the flab on her face. I mean, I wouldn't but—it's something I think about. (*Pause.*) When I was little I used to think I could talk to God. In fact, I thought I could talk to God better than anybody in the world and I didn't understand why world leaders didn't come to me to pray to God to solve the world's problems. I'd sit in church with my family. And my mother—my mother is a very beautiful woman. She looks like Italian women on jars of spaghetti sauce. And she's got big old bosoms. And I like 'em. And I don't care what that sounds like 'cause it's one of my favorite parts of my mother. (*Pause.*) And I remember when my father died, it, uh, she showed great dignity. She took my hand and she said, "You go take care of your sister now." And I said, "Who's gonna take care of you?" And she said, "I can take care of myself, you take care of your sister." And I said, "But I want to take care of you." And she said, "Look, you get in there and take care of your sister before I knock you into the middle of next week." And I did. And my sister was so pretty when she—was in her confirmation dress. (*Pause.*) Somebody's been flashing the nurses? I don't know anything about that. It wasn't me. (*Pause.*) It wasn't me.

Blackout

Transition 5.   Natwick letter.
Dear Mother. My friendship with Gately grows warmer and warmer. He is a very perceptive person for a semi-illiterate. Mother, he's never even read *The New Yorker*. I think he appreciates our little chats.

SCENE SIX.   Hemingway/Peaches.

Gately fixing radio.

NATWICK. (*Groaning.*) Another book on Hemingway.
GATELY. Hmm.
NATWICK. And yet, did he have the right to take his own life?
GATELY. Hmm.
NATWICK. Don't forget, he was no longer the man he once was.

GATELY. Who it, for Christ's sake?

NATWICK. I tell you, Gately, if I had any kind of courage at all, I'd go straight to my room, take out a razor and slash my wrists. Oh God, I wish I could.

GATELY. What's preventing you?

NATWICK. I use an electric.

GATELY. I'll lend you one of mine.

NATWICK. What kind of thing is that to say to a person?

GATELY. Well, if you really wanted to.

NATWICK. But I don't *really* want to.

GATELY. You don't.

NATWICK. No. Suicide is a plea for help.

GATELY. Well, I'm trying to help. I'll lend you the razor blade.

NATWICK. That's just great. A man reaches out to his fellow man, a hand reaches out into the darkness for a little comfort, a little compassion, I reach out—and you hand me a razor blade.

GATELY. Okay. I won't lend you the razor blade.

NATWICK. What's the matter? Don't you trust me?

GATELY. Yes.

NATWICK. You'll get it back.

GATELY. How? You'll be dead. You'll be stretched out on the floor—

NATWICK. Actually, a bath tub.

GATELY. Bath tub?

NATWICK. Gately, for instance, suppose I can't cope with the world when they let me out of here.

GATELY. You can get out any time you want to.

NATWICK. I know that. I see my suicide, Gately, as a beautiful thing. There I am in my mother's home, my wrists slashed, my blood filling the bath tub.

GATELY. But why a bath tub?

NATWICK. I don't want to make a mess.

GATELY. Why?

NATWICK. My mother would kill me.

GATELY. You'll be dead. She can't do anything to you then.

NATWICK. You don't know my mother. (*Pause.*) You know, you don't know what it's like growing up rich.

GATELY. You know—you're right.

NATWICK. When you're rich there's only one way to go—down.

16

GATELY. Same thing when you're poor. Only it's a different direction.

NATWICK. All my life, I've known I was going to fail. My mother had a brilliant career planned for me. Anything less than Secretary of State would have been considered a failure. I remember my childhood as a succession of summer homes moving farther and farther out on Long Island. My sense of failure grew in proportion to the size of the houses, each one larger than the last. When we got the place at Montauk, I joined the Army. Everyone was surprised that the Army took me. Including me.

GATELY. Isn't it funny how some days we can shoot the breeze like this and other days, we just can't talk at all.

NATWICK. There are good days and there are bad days. On good days, I can talk. On bad days—well, one dares not eat a peach as they say.

GATELY. Eat a peach. Why wouldn't a person dare eat a peach?

NATWICK. It's something someone once said.

GATELY. Who said it?

NATWICK. T. S. Eliot.

GATELY. T. S. Eliot was afraid to eat a peach?

NATWICK. Gately.

GATELY. Was he allergic to them?

NATWICK. Prufrock didn't dare to eat a peach.

GATELY. Was Prufrock allergic to them?

NATWICK. Prufrock is not a person. He's a poem.

GATELY. I know that. (Pause.) Why wouldn't he dare to eat a peach?

NATWICK. Because he was afraid.

GATELY. Was there something wrong with the peach? Had it gone bad.

NATWICK. There was nothing wrong with the peach.

GATELY. What was he afraid of then?

NATWICK. Life.

GATELY. Life?

NATWICK. Yes.

GATELY. He was so afraid of Life that he couldn't eat a peach? That's disgraceful!

NATWICK. It was the small things of life that defeated him. The momentary terrors.

GATELY. Like what?

17

NATWICK. Old age. Old women. Tea parties.

GATELY. Tea parties! Old women! Hell, that's just minor league stuff! I hope this Prufrock never runs into any of the MAJOR PROBLEMS OF LIFE. Then he really wouldn't be able to eat the peach!

NATWICK. Why are you getting so upset?

GATELY. Where'd he eat this peach?

NATWICK. On a beach.

GATELY. Well, that's just dandy. The guy's so sensitive he can't even eat a goddamn peach on a goddamn beach.

NATWICK. It's just a metaphor, Gately, okay?

GATELY. I just hope this guy doesn't get drafted, that's all I hope.

NATWICK. The guy can't get drafted. The guy's in a poem, Gately, you know what poems are?

GATELY. I read poems.

NATWICK. When?

GATELY. All the time! I read 'em till I'm sick of 'em.

NATWICK. What poems? Give me one.

GATELY. Hiawatha. It's a great poem! Look it up!

NATWICK. Well, it's like that.

GATELY. What is?

NATWICK. You can't draft Hiawatha.

GATELY. Even if you did, what makes you think he'd serve? Hiawatha was one of the greatest Indians of all time. What makes you think he'd fight for this shitty Army? He'd go to Canada first!

NATWICK. Are you saying Hiawatha was a draft dodger?

GATELY. Not if it was an Indian war. If it was an Indian war, hell, he'd put on his war paint, get in his canoe and go whip ass!

NATWICK. (*Weary.*) But only his own wars.

GATELY. That's right! And if everybody would fight their own private wars, things would be all right. But no, people have to keep sticking their noses into other people's wars! You see what I mean Natwick? You see what I'm trying to say?

NATWICK. No.

GATELY. The thing about the world is . . . the thing about the world is . . . the world is . . . you see what I'm trying to say?

NATWICK. And that's why I don't want to talk about it.

GATELY. (*Pause.*) You just can't stand to lose an argument. Can you?

NATWICK. (*As he exits.*) One, two, three—aaaah! (*Gately fixing radio. Off-stage we hear Silvio's voice.*)

SILVIO. Hey, gorgeous. Turn around. Ta-dah! Woo! (*Entering.*) Did you ever ask yourself the secret of my incredible sexual power over women?

GATELY. No.

SILVIO. Why the nurses can't resist me?

GATELY. The nurses hate you, Silvio.

SILVIO. Ah. That's what they would have you believe.

GATELY. They got me believin' it.

SILVIO. You wanna hear a great line for picking girls up?

GATELY. Sure.

SILVIO. Now this works best for Catholic girls.

GATELY. Okay.

SILVIO. You tell 'em you're a priest.

GATELY. A priest.

SILVIO. Okay. Look we'll set the scene. This is what they call settin' the scene. Now, you're sitting there. At the table. What can this table be?

GATELY. A table.

SILVIO. Okay. We'll make it a table. We're in a night club.

GATELY. Can it be a singles joint?

SILVIO. Gately, you been to a single joint?

GATELY. No.

SILVIO. Okay, I tell you what. In settin' the scene we'll make this a singles joint.

GATELY. (*Awed.*) Where'd you learn all this?

SILVIO. Once I hung around a USO group that was rehearsing. A Bob Hope thing. I tell you somethin', Gately . . .

GATELY. Yeah?

SILVIO. Never be afraid to mingle in the arts.

GATELY. All right!

SILVIO. Okay, so we're in a singles joint. And you're a broad. Everybody's being hustled. It's a fucking meat market!

GATELY. What's a nice girl like me doing in a place like this?

SILVIO. That's it! That's it! That's what's called gettin' into character!

GATELY. Am I lonely?

SILVIO. Are you lonely? A face like that. What do you think.

GATELY! I'm lonely, huh?

SILVIO. That's right. You're like ugly Catholic girls all over the world. You're like a different breed. You sit there being ugly, ruining life for everybody else.

GATELY. Are you lonely?

SILVIO. Gately! I'm a priest! Of course I'm lonely. I'm one of the loneliest, horniest guys on the face of the earth. OK, you're sitting there by yourself. So I come in. And I'm very depressed. So I come in and I look around. No, you don't see me yet, Gately. I see you. I come over and I say, "Pardon me, miss, is this seat taken?"

GATELY. Yes, it is.

SILVIO. What?

GATELY. Buzz off.

SILVIO. No. You don't say nothing.

GATELY. You want me to call the management?

SILVIO. That's not the way it goes.

GATELY. Male chauvinist pig.

SILVIO. Gately.

GATELY. What?

SILVIO. Don't give me such a hard time, OK?

GATELY. I just wanted to make it realistic.

SILVIO. Okay. But you're making it too realistic. We'll do it again. So I come in very depressed and—you don't see me yet, Gately—I see you and I come over and I say, "Pardon me, miss, but is this seat taken?"

GATELY. Well, why not.

SILVIO. Mind if I sit down?

GATELY. Well, why not.

SILVIO. May I order you another drink?

GATELY. Well, sure.

SILVIO. Bartender. Two more of the same. Do you mind if I smoke?

GATELY. Well, why not. (*Silvio takes out two cigarettes, puts them in his mouth, lights them both. He offers her one.*) I don't want it.

SILVIO. Why not?

GATELY. You've slobbered all over it.

SILVIO. No I haven't.

GATELY. You've had it in your mouth.

SILVIO. Gately, take the fuckin' cigarette. (*Gately takes the cigarette.*) I hope you won't think I'm being too personal but . . . what's your name.

GATELY. Woodruff Gately.

SILVIO. Woodruff?

GATELY. Woodruff.

SILVIO. I've never known a girl named Woodruff before.

GATELY. You've never known a girl like me.

SILVIO. If I seem a little nervous, it's because I don't usually come to this kind of place. Have you ever come to this kind of place?

GATELY. I'm a Baptist.

SILVIO. You must be very lonely.

GATELY. Why, because I'm a Baptist?

SILVIO. (*Putting his hand on Gately's leg.*) Can I tell you something very personal.

GATELY. Okay. But don't get smutty.

SILVIO. I just wanted to tell you that I don't get a chance to meet beautiful women. You see, actually, I'm a priest.

GATELY. Well, I don't get a chance to meet men. You see, actually, I'm a lesbian.

SILVIO. (*Gets up angrily.*) That's it! Forget it, Gately.

GATELY. I'm sorry!

SILVIO. No! No! Let's just forget it. I try to teach you something! Give you the benefit of my experience, my life! You know what you are. I'll tell you what you are. A fucking ingrate, that's what you are. Why'd you make her a lesbian?

GATELY. I don't know.

SILVIO. Not even a priest could pick up a lesbian. Nobody could pick up a lesbian.

GATELY. A lesbian could!

SILVIO. Who cares! That does me no good. I can't become a lesbian every time I wanna get laid.

GATELY. No.

SILVIO. You see my point.

GATELY. You could become a transvestite.

SILVIO. What?

GATELY. Wear women's clothes.

SILVIO. But I don't want to wear women's clothes.

GATELY. I know you don't.

SILVIO. I know I don't, too.

21

GATELY. You want to wear a kilt.

SILVIO. That's right.

GATELY. Which is nearly women's clothes.

SILVIO. (*Pause.*) You know something, Gately? At the rate you're going, you may never get laid.

Blackout

Transition 6.

GATELY. Silvio.

SILVIO. What, Gately.

GATELY. What is a seven-letter word for hemorrhoidal tissue?

SILVIO. Nat-wick. N-A-T-W-I-C-K.

SCENE SEVEN. The Cup.

Gately fixing a radio. Natwick enters in near panic.

NATWICK. Gately, you've got to help me.

GATELY. I'm busy.

NATWICK. Gately, this is a matter of life and death.

GATELY. I'm busy.

NATWICK. Gately, would you look at me! (*Natwick lifts hand from pocket secretively. He holds a cup in his hand. He lowers hand back into his pocket.*)

GATELY. Natwick, you've got a cup in your pocket.

NATWICK. Yes.

GATELY. Why do you have a cup in your pocket?

NATWICK. Actually, I've got a cup glued to my hand in my pocket.

GATELY. Why would you glue a cup to your hand?

NATWICK. You idiot! I didn't do it! Silvio did it! He handed me a cup of coffee and suddenly I was glued. (*Gately tries, unsuccessfully, to disengage Natwick from the cup.*)

GATELY. (*Fascinated.*) Let's see. He must have used that super epoxy glue. You know it dries in five seconds?

NATWICK. Yes, I know.

GATELY. I always wondered if this stuff would work.

NATWICK. Yes, well, it works.

22

GATELY. You better take that over to the shop.

NATWICK. I'm going to find an orderly.

GATELY. Why? You'll get Silvio in trouble.

NATWICK. I *want* to get Silvio in trouble.

GATELY. Natwick! You've got to understand. Silvio's wound has left him emotionally scarred.

NATWICK. You want emotional scars? I have a urine bag strapped to my side. You think that's fun? Going through life as a portable toilet?

GATELY. Silvio's wound is different.

NATWICK. I don't want to hear about Silvio's wound.

GATELY. Natwick.

NATWICK. I don't want to hear about Silvio's wound. I'm going to find an orderly.

GATELY. You do and Silvio'll kill you.

NATWICK. What kind of wound was it?

GATELY. Shrapnel.

NATWICK. Well. Shrapnel. That's not so bad.

GATELY. It blew off his testicles and his penis.

NATWICK. Wow. That explains a lot. Sure. He flashes the nurses to assert his lack of manhood.

GATELY. Sure! That explains the flashing!

NATWICK. It explains his macho act.

GATELY. Sure. It explains the macho act.

NATWICK. It explains everything.

GATELY. It even explains the cup.

NATWICK. No, it doesn't explain the cup.

GATELY. No. I guess he just hates your guts.

NATWICK. Yeah. That explains the cup.

GATELY. (*Pause.*) What're you gonna do?

NATWICK. I don't know. Things can't go on like this. First they hang a urine bag on me. Now a cup. It's like I'm a Christmas tree.

GATELY. Why don't you make friends with Silvio?

NATWICK. How disgusting. (*Pause.*) What do I have to do?

GATELY. First of all, loosen up. You make people nervous.

NATWICK. Why.

GATELY. You're uptight.

NATWICK. I am not uptight!

GATELY. You stand like you got a rod up your ass.

NATWICK. I'm from Great Neck.

23

GATELY. Here. Look. Snap your fingers. Act like you're cool. (*Natwick does so. Mechanically.*) You look like someone put a quarter in you. Say, "Hey man, what's happening."

NATWICK. Hey man, what's happening?

GATELY. (*Pause.*) OK. We'll come back to that. (*Pause.*) I know. You've got to take an interest in Silvio's hobbies.

NATWICK. Like what? Child molesting?

GATELY. No. Mainly flashing nurses, kilts, men's underwear.

NATWICK. Men's underwear?

GATELY. Yes, that and—oh, here he comes.

NATWICK. I think I'm going to be sick (*Silvio enters in a hurry.*)

GATELY. Hey Silvio, what's happenin', man?

SILVIO. Gately . . .

NATWICK. Hey Silvio, what's happenin', man?

SILVIO. Gately, I gotta talk to you.

GATELY. Sure, Silvio, but Natwick just said hello to you.

NATWICK. Hey Silvio, what's happenin', man?

SILVIO. (*Pause.*) Gately, it's Nurse O'Brian. She's been trans-ferred. All week I been planning on flashing her. I got her on the list for Tuesday.

GATELY. So?

SILVIO. Today is Tuesday.

NATWICK. Oh man, what a bummer.

SILVIO. What's a matter with him?

NATWICK. Hey, Silvio: "What it *is* baby?"

SILVIO. Why's he talking like a spade?

NATWICK. I mean what is this *jive* about O'Brian leaving.

SILVIO. Jesus. What is your problem, Natwick?

NATWICK. No problem, baby.

SILVIO. Don't call me baby.

NATWICK. I think it's great the way you flash nurses. You got it down to an art form.

SILVIO. Exposing yourself is not an art form. It's disgusting. You ever flashed anyone, Natwick?

NATWICK. No.

SILVIO. So what do you know about it.

NATWICK. Nothing.

SILVIO. That's right. Gately . . .

NATWICK. Hey Silvio, you wanna know what kind of underwear I'm wearing?

SILVIO. Do I what?

24

NATWICK. Very tight jockey shorts.
SILVIO. (*Backing off.*) Hey, has he gone queer or somethin'?
Jesus. First O'Brian gets transferred, now Natwick goes queer.
Jesus.
NATWICK. Silvio—
SILVIO. Keep your hands to yourself, Natwick.
NATWICK. I just want to be your friend.
SILVIO. You remember the cup? I'll glue you, Natwick. I swear to
God I'll glue you.
NATWICK. (*Terrified.*) Don't glue me! Don't glue me! Don't
glue me!
SILVIO. Hey. It's just a little glue. (*Exits.*)
GATELY. Well. You blew it.

Blackout

Transition 7.

GATELY. Silvio.
SILVIO. What?
GATELY. If you had one wish, what would it be?
SILVIO. I'd like to be on Johnny Carson.
GATELY. Why?
SILVIO. I might meet Charo.

SCENE EIGHT.   Radio Parts Are Disappearing.

Gately fixing radio. Silvio with baseball glove.

SILVIO. Gately. How can you work for weeks on one radio?
GATELY. You've got to keep the incoming parts ahead of the out-
going parts.
SILVIO. What?
GATELY. (*Looking around.*) Silvio. Radio parts are disappearing.
SILVIO. When?
GATELY. All the time.
SILVIO. You think someone's stealing them?
GATELY. Possibly.
SILVIO. You could be losing them.
GATELY. Possibly. Anyway I have to replace the missing parts.
SILVIO. Where do you get the missing parts?

GATELY. You can't just get parts. You have to steal the entire radio.

SILVIO. From where?

GATELY. Administration.

SILVIO. . . . How many radios have you stolen?

GATELY. To date. 27.

SILVIO. I see.

GATELY. I'm not discouraged. The main thing is to keep your incoming parts ahead of your outgoing parts. America was built on this theory. Silvio. The Free Enterprise System. And if one guy like me can make a radio work—then America works.

SILVIO. Interesting theory.

GATELY. It's simple really. It's just a question of incoming parts and outgoing parts.

SILVIO. Gately . . . I wish you luck.

GATELY. Silvio, thank you. (*They shake hands. Gately goes back to radio. Silvio steals a part.*)

Blackout

Transition 8.   Natwick letter.

NATWICK. Dear Mother. Thank you for sending the guppies for my aquarium. However, please do not send anymore, because Silvio took them out last night and smashed all my guppies with a ballpeen hammer. Please send socks.

SCENE NINE.   Jack Palance.

Natwick alone. Silvio enters, unseen, comes up behind Natwick. Silvio is acting very strange.

SILVIO. Hello, Natwick.

NATWICK. (*Startled.*) I wish you wouldn't do that.

SILVIO. Where's Gately?

NATWICK. He's obviously not here.

SILVIO. Good. We can have a little chat.

NATWICK. (*Rising.*) I really don't—

SILVIO. Sit down.

NATWICK. Thank you. (*Pause.*)

26

SILVIO. Well, it's been lovely getting to know you this spring, Natwick.

NATWICK. Yes, I haven't know fun like this since the Tet Offensive.

SILVIO. You weren't no grunt. (*Pause.*) You were a clerk.

NATWICK. Correct. (*Pause.*) Silvio, are you stoned? Are you stoned? That's good 'cause when you're stoned you mellow out? Right? Mellow?

SILVIO. You know who people tell me I look like?

NATWICK. No.

SILVIO. Jack Palance.

NATWICK. There is a certain resemblance.

SILVIO. Thing is, I had this dream the other night about Jack Palance. I dreamed Jack Palance was the leader of a girl scout troop. And he was dressed like a girl scout. And you and me and Gately where members of this girl scout troop. And we knew Jack Palance was going to do something horribile to us . . . so we decided to sneak up on him. And it was dark, Natwick, very, very dark. And then we opened the door. And there in this room was Jack Palance in this huge green girl scout uniform. And all around wer dead girl scouts. He had bitten off their heads and drained their blood. (*Pause.*) Well, what do you think of this dream?

NATWICK. Fascinating.

SILVIO. Yeah, I know. But I mean in the Freudian sense.

NATWICK. Oh. In a Freudian sense, I'd say it was very common.

SILVIO. Common.

NATWICK. Oh yes. I think everyone's had that dream. I know I have. (*Pause.*)

SILVIO. You're from Long Island.

NATWICK. That's right.

SILVIO. Great Neck.

NATWICK. That's right.

SILVIO. Bet you had the shirts with the little alligators on them.

NATWICK. Uh, huh.

SILVIO. Bet you had a summer home in the Hamptons.

NATWICK. Montauk, actually.

SILVIO. Montauk, actually. (*Pause.*) I picture your home overlooking the ocean. The water coming in and out. In and out. In and out.

NATWICK. That's the way it is when everything's working right.

27

SILVIO. You pussy.

NATWICK. What.

SILVIO. I'll bet your mother played mah jong by the sea.

NATWICK. What's my mother . . .

SILVIO. And you went to private schools where they all wore the alligator shirts.

NATWICK. Silvio. (*Silvio takes out a knife. Puts it under Natwick's neck, stands him up.*) Silvio. Don't. (*Silvio releases Natwick and walks off.*)

Blackout

Transition 9.   Over intercom.

General announcement for all patients. Radios are being stolen from Administration. This is counter productive to the effort. This can't go on. Repeat. This can't go on.

SCENE TEN.   I Can't Go On.

Gately fixing radio. Silvio listening to radio.

GATELY. (*Rising.*) I can't go on! I'll never fix this fucking radio!

SILVIO. (*Going to him.*) What seems to be the trouble here, trooper?

GATELY. (*Near tears.*) I try and I try and nothing ever gets done!

SILVIO. Calm down. Take two deep breaths. (*Gately takes them.*) Now then, tell me what your problem is here.

GATELY. It's that damn radio. I'll never get it fixed. Parts keep disappearing! Silvio, there's something wrong with me. Here. In my head. I think I'm—

SILVIO. Hey, you're just having a bad day.

GATELY. I am?

SILVIO. Sure. Did I ever tell you the story of the first day when I realized there was something wrong with me? That I needed help?

GATELY. No.

SILVIO. Well, I woke up one morning in Cleveland. I was living with me sister at the time. It was a beautiful day. I looked out the window. And I remember thinking, Ohio is a party dip. Not long after I attacked my fellow workers with a tire tool.

28

GATELY. Did you do that?

SILVIO. Sure I did that.

GATELY. But you're psychotic.

SILVIO. Exactly my point. And see, I couldn't even repair a radio.

GATELY. Well, it's not easy.

SILVIO. Hell no, it's not.

GATELY. Radios are complicated things.

SILVIO. Of course, they are.

GATELY. They're a product of human evolution.

SILVIO. Gately. If there's one thing that's clear to us at this point in time, it is that man is making progress. Now, are you going to let yourself be defeated by an inanimate object? You are not. You are going to go over there and fix that radio.

GATELY. Will you go with me?

SILVIO. Of course, I will. (*They go to table. Gately sits.*) Are you ready to resume?

GATELY. I am.

SILVIO. As you do, remember: "The flesh of man can be torn, beaten and destroyed, but the human spirit abideth forever and shall not perish."

GATELY. Who said that?

SILVIO. Casey Stengal. (*Gately works. Silvio steals another part.*)

Blackout

Transition 10. Silvio—Psychiatrist.

PSYCHIATRIST. Silvio do you realize you're afraid of women?

SILVIO. Look Doc, I'm not afraid of women.

PSYCHIATRIST. Silvio, you're afraid of women.

SILVIO. I'm not afraid of women.

PSYCHIATRIST. Silvio, are you *nervous* around women?

SILVIO. Oh well *yeah,* maybe I'm nervous around women. (*Pause.*) You didn't *say* nervous.

SCENE ELEVEN. Krullick.

Gately fixing radio. Silvio enters humming to himself.

SILVIO. How are you this afternoon Woodruff. My what a lovely day.

GATELY. You feeling all right, Silvio?

SILVIO. Of course, I'm all right.

GATELY. You've got that look on your face.

SILVIO. What look?

GATELY. The last time you had that look, you flushed the cherry bombs down the toilet.

SILVIO. Gately, I'm in love.

GATELY. I don't want to hear about your love life, Silvio.

SILVIO. Don't you want to know with who?

GATELY. No.

SILVIO. Nurse Krullick.

GATELY. Not Neanderthal Krullick. (*Silvio nods.*) She's the ugliest woman in the world.

SILVIO. Do you really think so?

GATELY. She's uglier than the guy in Ben Hur that got dragged behind the chariot.

SILVIO. You think so.

GATELY. Of course. At least the guy that had been drug around by the chariot had an excuse. But Krullick was born that way.

SILVIO. That's why she deserves my love more than the rest.

GATELY. What.

SILVIO. Ugly women appreciate love more. They want it more. Gately, there are thousands of women out there that are starved for love.

GATELY. Silvio, Silvio. You're so fickle.

SILVIO. Fickle? Me?

GATELY. Only last week you were depressed because time was running out for you to make it with Elizabeth Taylor.

SILVIO. A mere infatuation. How can you compare Elizabeth Taylor with Krullick?

GATELY. It's not easy. (*Natwick enters. Sits.*)

SILVIO. Good afternoon, Natwick.

NATWICK. Uh . . . good afternoon.

SILVIO. Is that a new robe?

NATWICK. No. It's the same one I've been wearing all spring.

SILVIO. Well, it looks very nice on you. (*Silvio walks away looking off.*)

NATWICK. What's the matter with him?

GATELY. He's in love.

NATWICK. Who's the lucky girl?

GATELY. Nurse Krullick.

NATWICK. Not Neanderthal Krullick. She's the ugliest woman in the world.

GATELY. Do you think she's uglier than the guy in Ben Hur that got dragged behind the chariot?

NATWICK. Oh of course.

SILVIO. Gately, this is it. Wish me luck.

GATELY. Good luck. What am I wishing you luck for?

SILVIO. I'm going to talk to Krullick.

GATELY. How? I don't think she speaks English.

SILVIO. I'm going to tell her exactly how I feel.

GATELY. That you love her?

SILVIO. Yes.

GATELY. Silvio, be careful. If Krullick thinks you're making fun of her she'll tear you limb from limb.

SILVIO. That's a chance I gotta take.

GATELY. Silvio . . . good luck. (*They shake hands solemnly.*)

NATWICK. Silvio— (*Natwick flashes Silvio the thumbs up sign. Silvio returns it. Silvio exits.*)

GATELY. Did you hear the news about Silvio? Silvio's leaving soon.

NATWICK. What?

GATELY. He's going to live with his sister in Cleveland.

NATWICK. Well . . . that's great.

GATELY. Yeah. Isn't that great?

NATWICK. How's the radio?

GATELY. Won't be long now. (*Natwick steals a radio part.*) Is it possible Silvio really loves Krullick?

NATWICK. It's possible.

GATELY. And that she loves him.

NATWICK. Well, its really a question of being faithful.

GATELY. (*Thoughtfully.*) People can be faithful to one another. It's hard. But they can do it. (*Pause.*) The coyote does it . . .

NATWICK. What?

GATELY. The coyote mates for life. He's entirely faithful. He doesn't fool around. And he's got plenty of chances. I mean—he's out there, under the stars, under the moon. And I'll bet he gets lonely. He howls.

NATWICK. Dolphins too. They mate for life!

GATELY. Do they?

NATWICK. I think so. I think they do!

GATELY. Good for them.

NATWICK. It just goes to show you, Gately.

GATELY. What?

NATWICK. Love is a many splendored thing.

GATELY. Why . . . that's beautiful. Love is a many splendored thing. Did you make that up, Natwick?

NATWICK. Yes I did, Gately.

GATELY. I'm impressed. (*Silvio enters quickly.*)

SILVIO. I can't fuckin' believe it.

GATELY. What?

SILVIO. I can't fucking believe it. I was standing there waiting for Krullick over by the cafeteria.

GATELY. Yeah.

SILVIO. And I saw her coming.

NATWICK. Yeah.

SILVIO. And I was about to say something to her, when suddenly out of nowhere comes Gleason. And what do you think the son of a bitch has the nerve to do?

GATELY. What?

SILVIO. He flashes Krullick.

NATWICK. Gleason flashes Krullick!

SILVIO. Can you believe that son of a bitch right in front of my very eyes! He flashes my Krullick!

GATELY. What? You give him a shot?

SILVIO. I was going to, but he turned around and hauled ass.

NATWICK. Gleason got away from you?

SILVIO. Gleason can move that wheelchair when he wants to.

NATWICK. Did you tell Krullick you loved her?

SILVIO. Natwick! Have a little sensitivity would you? The woman had just been flashed by a horny paraplegic. Romance was the last thing she had on her mind. (*Pause.*)

NATWICK. I hear you're leaving soon.

SILVIO. Yeah. That's right . . . tomorrow.

GATELY. (*Shocked.*) Tomorrow?

SILVIO. I was gonna tell you. My schedule got pushed up.

NATWICK. Guess you'll be glad to get back?

SILVIO. Fuckin 'a. Y'know, see the old neighborhood. Check it out.

GATELY. (*Trying to smile.*) Well, we'll give you a going away party.

32

SILVIO. Yeah. Sure. Look. I gotta go pack and everything. See you later. (*Gately and Natwick watch Silvio go out.*)

Blackout

Transition 11.

NATWICK. Hello there! This is your entertainment director Pfc. Natwick. Tonight's movie is *Bigger Than Life.* (1956) Starring James Mason. The frightening story of a cortisone addict. (*We hear an audience groaning.*) It's very well acted. (*An audience booing.*) Barbara Rush is *very* good. (*An audience heckling.*)

SCENE TWELVE. The Party

Gately and Silvio are very drunk. A bottle of Canadian Club and two glasses are out on the table.

SILVIO. I mean, am I right or am I right?
GATELY. You're right.
SILVIO. You're damn right I'm right. (*Pause.*) What're we talking about?
GATELY. Cleveland.
SILVIO. Yeah. I just don't want it to be like last time.
GATELY. Last time you attacked your fellow workers with a tire tool.
SILVIO. I know. (*Pause.*) Say, where's the asshole?
GATELY. Natwick's been in his room all day.
SILVIO. How come?
GATELY. (*Delicately.*) I think he's depressed 'cause you're leaving. (*Pause.*) You know Natwick.
SILVIO. Yeah.
GATELY. You worried about going to Cleveland tomorrow?
SILVIO. No . . . well . . . yeah . . . a little.
GATELY. What're you worried about?
SILVIO. I'm worried about that damned Protestant.
GATELY. What?
SILVIO. My sister married a Protestant. I mean, how do you talk to a Protestant?
GATELY. I'm a Protestant.

SILVIO. You're different. (*Natwick enters. He has been drinking heavily.*)

NATWICK. (*Despairing.*) A party. Of course. I might have known. No one invites me anywhere.

GATELY. Natwick, you know perfectly well I invited you.

NATWICK. I couldn't hear you. The door was locked.

SILVIO. What were you doing in there, Natwick? Holding your breath?

NATWICK. That's right! Insult me! I just came out here to give you this. (*Hands Silvio a letter.*)

SILVIO. It's from my sister. (*He begins to open it.*) I'll read it later. (*Pause.*)

NATWICK. Well, don't anybody offer me a drink.

SILVIO. OK, we won't.

NATWICK. Who needs your party!

GATELY. C'mon, sit down here, Natwick. I've got a surprise for you guys.

NATWICK. I've got martinis in my room. I have many martinis in my room.

GATELY. Sit over here, Natwick.

SILVIO. I think he's drunk.

NATWICK. I am not drunk.

SILVIO. Tell the truth, Natwick. You drunk?

NATWICK. Go fuck yourself.

SILVIO. Natwick is *very* drunk.

NATWICK. I am not. Gimme a drink.

GATELY. OK. Wait. We don't have enough glasses.

NATWICK. That's all right. I brought my own. (*He lifts hand out of pocket. A cup is glued to it.*)

GATELY. (*Reprovingly.*) Silvio.

SILVIO. (*Good-naturedly.*) Hey—a going away present. (*Silvio and Natwick are seated on opposite sides of the table.*)

GATELY. Now, put on your party hats. (*He gives them their party hats.*)

NATWICK. Oh boy, party hats!

SILVIO. Jesus Christ, do we have to?

GATELY. Yes.

NATWICK. (*Wrestling with his hat.*) Jesus Christ.

GATELY. Here. I'll give you a hand.

NATWICK. It's all his fault! Can't even put a party hat on.

GATELY. (*Adjusting hat.*) There. (*Becoming quite solemn.*) I suppose you're wondering why we're gathered here this evening?

SILVIO. To wear these little hats?

GATELY. We're gathered here to say farewell and good fortune to our friend Silvio.

NATWICK. (*Giving a raspberry.*) FFFTTT.

GATELY. And to celebrate the completion of the radio.

SILVIO. (*Sober.*) What?

NATWICK. (*Sober.*) What?

SILVIO. Have you tried it?

GATELY. Not yet.

SILVIO. How do you know it's gonna work?

GATELY. I've decided it will.

SILVIO. Radios are very complicated things. Remember we talked about this.

GATELY. I know, but I've worked long enough on this. I can't work on this thing the rest of my life. So today I screwed up the back and said to hell with it. It's now or never.

SILVIO. It's never.

GATELY. What?

SILVIO. There's no way that radio can work.

GATELY. Why not.

SILVIO. Because I've been stealing radio parts.

GATELY. You? I knew it! I knew something was happening. Do you know how many radios I've had to steal to replace those parts?

NATWICK. I took some, too.

GATELY. You what? Do you know what this means? Do you have any *idea?*

SILVIO. It means the radio won't work.

GATELY. It's true people are always stealing from me. It's horrible. I leave my room in the morning and when I return in the evening it's been stripped bare. Last week someone stole my dirty clothes. Stole my dirty underwear. (*Pause.*) All my life people stole from me. Bicycles. Baseball cards. My shoes. Shit. (*Silence. Suddenly Gately gives out a loud . . .*) I'm through being stole from! That's it. No more stealing from old Gately! That's it. No more stealing. From now . . . on I'm giving it away! Take my shoes. (*Takes off slippers.*) Take my shirt! (*Takes off shirt.*) Take my pants! (*Takes off pants.*) Take it all! Damn vultures. (*Stands in rage and defiance in his socks and underwear.*)

35

NATWICK. Can we have your socks?

GATELY. Take the damn things. (*Takes off socks. Stares at the radio.*) And take the goddamn radio. (*He goes to the radio with savage intensity. Grasps it, lifts it over his head. Is about to smash it into a million piaces when, miraculously it comes on playing very loudly "The National Emblem March." The scene turns from one or pain to one of dazzled awe. Softly, Gately places the radio on the table. Turns off radio.*)

SILVIO. Gately . . . you fixed the radio. You know what this means, don't you? (*Gately nods.*) So. When you thinking of getting out of here?

GATELY. (*Quietly.*) When they let me out.

SILVIO. You can get out anytime you want.

GATELY. I know. (*Pause.*)

SILVIO. Say, Gately, where you from?

GATELY. Georgia.

SILVIO. I know that, but where. What did you do there?

GATELY. Started out on a red dirt farm near Macon with my old man. He was a funny old guy. Big old hands. He couldn't seem to make nothing work. He fucked up everything he touched. He fucked up the farm, he fucked up runnin' a fruit stand. He fucked up workin' for the state. Finally we moved to Birmingham. He said that's where people like them moved to when they'd fucked up everything. He went to work in textiles. One day I come home and there he was in the middle of the afternoon leaned up against the house. Them big old hands. That's khen I joined the Army. I couldn't stand to see him fuck up no more.

SILVIO. Say, Gately, when you were a kid, you ever do the Tarzan yell?

GATELY. Sure. Everyone did the Tarzan yell.

NATWICK. I never did.

GATELY. Why?

NATWICK. I had asthma.

SILVIO. Stand up here, Gately. I'm gonna show you how to do the Tarzan yell.

GATELY. Hell. I bet I do it better than you.

SILVIO. Are you fuckin' kiddin' me?

GATELY. I ain't kiddin' you.

SILVIO. I used to win prizes doing the yell.

GATELY. Big deal.

SILVIO. I did the Tarzan yell at a Bar Mitzvah once.

NATWICK. Hm. Must have been reform.

GATELY. OK. Who goes first.

SILVIO. I go first. Give you something to shoot for. (*He does the yell.*)

GATELY. I'm not impressed. (*He does the yell. Unexpectedly Natwick does the call.*)

SILVIO. (*Realization.*) Natwick.

NATWICK. (*Pause.*) I did the Tarzan yell. I did the Tarzan yell.

SILVIO. This calls for a drink. (*They pour drinks, solemnly.*) A toast . . . to Tarzan.

ALL. To Tarzan. (*They drink.*)

GATELY. To Cheetah.

ALL. To Cheetah. (*They drink and sit.*)

GATELY. Sometimes I wished we were in a jungle somewhere.

NATWICK. (*Nodding.*) You know all over Africa, apes and other wild things that climb are falling out of trees at an unprecendented rate.

SILVIO. Why?

NATWICK. Civilization. There's no place anymore for wild and wounded animals. There's just all sorts of ancient things that disappear. They get obsolete. Like the dodo bird. And elephants.

GATELY. And Indians.

NATWICK. And Indians.

GATELY. And salmon.

SILVIO. And grilse.

NATWICK. Did you know that the universe is collapsing? That's right. The universe is collapsing. The energy in stars eventually collapses in on themselves. Eventually the entire universe will collapse in on itself.

SILVIO. Where will it go?

NATWICK. Nowhere.

GATELY. What will be left?

NATWICK. Nothing.

SILVIO. No. There's gotta be something left.

NATWICK. Nope.

GATELY. A couple of little planets.

NATWICK. Not even a little card table and a little radio.

SILVIO. At least there'll be a lot of open space for development.

NATWICK. No. When stars collapse, they create a vacuum and suck space into it.

GATELY. There won't even be any space? (*Natwick shakes his head.*)

SILVIO. Jesus Christ, Natwick, no wonder you don't get invited to parties. You are the most depressive son-of-a-bitch that ever lived.

GATELY. He's an asshole.

SILVIO. Gately! You've admitted it! You've finally admitted that Natwick is an asshole!

GATELY. Yes.

SILVIO. Now I can die happy.

NATWICK. Big deal. He admits I'm an asshole. I *am* an asshole. Even I'll admit that.

SILVIO. Natwick . . . even you will admit you're an asshole?

NATWICK. Of course.

SILVIO. That's wonderful! Let's all say it out loud. Natwick is an asshole.

ALL. Natwick is an asshole.

SILVIO. Louder.

ALL. Natwick is an asshole!

SILVIO. One more time!!

ALL. Natwick is an asshole! Gately is an asshole! Silvio . . . Silvio is an asshole. (*A contented silence.*)

SILVIO. Natwick. How long is it gonna take for everything to start collapsing in on itself?

NATWICK. Oh, trillions and trillions of years.

SILVIO. Natwick, then there's nothing to worry about.

NATWICK. There's not? OK. Goodnight.

SILVIO. I'm gonna be in Cleveland tomorrow. (*Reads letter.*) "My darling brother . . ."

GATELY. Look, Silvio, the sun's coming up.

> By the shores of Gitchiegoomie
> By the shining big sea waters.
> At the doorway of his wigwam
> In the pleasant summer morning
> Hiawatha stood and waited.
> All the air was full of freshness.
> All the earth was bright and joyous.

Natwick, you awake.

NATWICK. Hm. Aarg.

GATELY. Look at the dawn, Natwick. When was the last time you were up this early?

NATWICK. Last week.

GATELY. Yeah?

NATWICK. I had diarrhea. (*Gately sees Silvio.*)

GATELY. Good morning, Silvio. See how the world looks this early. All dewy. It's like Eden, Silvio. Listen. It's like Eden.

SILVIO. My sister don't want me. She's gonna have the Protestant's kid.

NATWICK. (*Pause.*) I'm sorry, Silvio.

SILVIO. (*Miserably.*) Yeah.

GATELY. Try not to be so miserable, Silvio.

SILVIO. Lately, I'm a fucking psychotic with his pecker blown off.

GATELY. Things could be worse.

SILVIO. How? How could things possibly be worse?

NATWICK. It could rain.

SILVIO. Lemme tell you guys somethin'. Big news flash. Whether it rains or not really doesn't make that much difference. It wouldn't change anything.

GATELY. It would ruin a perfectly nice day. Look at it, Silvio! This day is special. It's like no other day that's ever been. It's like no other day that ever will be. This day will never come again.

SILVIO. Promise?

Slow blackout

PROPERTY LIST

On Stage:
Disassembled radio
Table
Chairs (3)

Off Stage:
Pocket notebook (Silvio)
Newspaper (Natwick)
Cigarettes & matches (Silvio)
Cup (to be glued to hand) (Natwick)
Baseball glove (Silvio)
Knife (Silvio)
Bottle of whiskey & 3 glasses
Letter (Natwick)
Party hats (3)